IMAGES OF ENGLAND

AMERSHAM

IMAGES OF ENGLAND

AMERSHAM

COLIN J. SEABRIGHT

TEMPUS

Frontispiece: This 1906 view past the Market Hall includes the end cottages of Church Row beyond the bowler-hatted huntsmen gathering in Market Square for their traditional Boxing Day meet.

First published 2004

Tempus Publishing Limited
The Mill, Brimscombe Port,
Stroud, Gloucestershire, GL5 2QG
www.tempus-publishing.com

© Colin J. Seabright, 2004

The right of Colin J. Seabright to be identified as the Author
of this work has been asserted in accordance with the
Copyrights, Designs and Patents Act 1988.

British Library Cataloguing in Publication Data.
A catalogue record for this book is available from the British Library.

ISBN 0 7524 3245 1

Typesetting and origination by Tempus Publishing Limited.
Printed in Great Britain by Midway Colour Print, Wiltshire.

Contents

Amersham High Street, pictured here in 1930, has been described as 'one of the finest medieval thoroughfares in England, a living museum of sixteenth- and seventeenth-century architecture', although many of the frontages actually date from the eighteenth century, added by the wealthier residents who wanted their homes to have a more fashionable appearance.

Acknowledgements

All the pictures, most of which are from postcards, come from my own collection, but I must express my gratitude to George Ward and all the other, anonymous, local photographers whose work was printed on postcards between about 1895 and 1955, and also the Baker family, whose 1928 family photo album I was able to purchase when it came up for sale a few years ago. I sincerely apologise if I have unwittingly infringed outstanding copyright on any of these pictures, but I believe all such rights to have expired.

Introduction

This little volume makes no pretence as a history of the town (for which I would recommend the comprehensive work by Julian Hunt, Bucks County Heritage Manager), nor as a guide, but is a selection of twentieth-century pictures of Amersham buildings, events and views, with scraps of relevant history and descriptions.

In the middle of the nineteenth century, various proposals had been made for a railway through Amersham, but they were blocked by the Drake family, who disliked the idea of trains in the valley spoiling the view from their Shardeloes home. Eventually the Metropolitan Railway planned a route along the ridge of Amersham Common, which met their objections by completely avoiding Shardeloes and the old town. Opened to Chalfont Road (and Chesham) in 1889 and to Amersham three years later, the stations on the high ground soon became centres for new housing and shops, thus saving the old town from the pressures of development which blighted most of the countryside near London. This, together with the Drake family's enlightened ownership of most of Old Amersham (until 1928), meant that the appearance of the town was effectively conserved long before the idea of conservation areas was even conceived; no new buildings were erected in the twentieth century in High Street, where the telegraph wires were routed behind the houses to keep the street free of poles.

A cyclists' touring guide to Buckinghamshire in the 1890s, describing Amersham as part of the route from London to Aylesbury, noted that 'The entrance into the town is through a broad street, which runs to the quaint market house, where it contracts to ordinary dimensions. There are a good many old houses in Amersham, of which the most striking are the Almshouses on the left leaving the town, and Little Shardeloes, a beautiful gabled building a little further on the same side of the road. After Amersham the road runs under the trees of Shardeloes, the seat of the Drakes, a historic estate dating from the time of Henry III. The house is in the heavy style of the Georges and replaces a fine Elizabethan building. The grounds are delightful, and within them is a handsome sheet of water, formed by a broadening of the Misbourne.'

At the start of the twentieth century, Amersham was already a thriving country town of some 2,600 inhabitants (including, as the county directory points out, eight officials and 128 inmates of the workhouse). The old town in the valley, then governed by a Rural District Council, had all modern conveniences, including over fifty shops, mains water and gas supplied by local companies, and a railway service from the new station just outside the town on the hill, where there was very little else but a few old cottages and farms among the fields around the old common and the first dozen or so buildings of the new town.

The arrival of the railway brought residents to the new town on the hill, and many visitors to the old, and a 1910 guide to 'Where to Live Round London' briefly sums up the area thus: 'Amersham town nestles peacefully in a hollow of the Chiltern Hills, and is surrounded by verdant slopes and wood-crowned heights. Its charm becomes apparent as one descends the long, steep hill from the railway station to the town. Around the station has sprung up quite a new town. On the summit of the hill here, which commands views over miles of the beautiful surrounding country, have been and are being erected pretty villas of varying character and size. These high lands are very healthy, the air being particularly pure and bracing. The old town is full of interest, its main street stretches for a mile or so along the main road from London to Aylesbury, and, with its ancient houses and inns, wears a delightfully picturesque aspect. Midway stands the old Town Hall, a handsome red-brick building with tiled roof, surmounted by a clock tower and bell lantern, erected in 1682 by Sir William Drake. Its arched and pillared lower floor long served as a market house, but there is no longer any market here, though the bell is always rung at noon on Tuesdays as of old.'

The market bell tradition eventually died out in 1940, but the Tuesday market has since been revived and transferred, together with most of the town's commercial activity, to Amersham on the Hill. The peak period of growth of the new Amersham was from 1910-60, and at Little Chalfont generally ten years later.

In the late 1920s and early '30s, the Metropolitan Railway, in a bid to encourage homeseekers to live in the area, and thus increase the number of commuters on its trains, coined the name 'Metroland' for the rural end of the line, and published annual guides, aimed also at the casual visitor or day-tripper. The following note is taken from the 1932 issue of *Metroland*: 'There are two Amershams, the old and the new. The old country town which, till disfranchised in 1832, returned a member to Parliament, lies snug in the valley of the Misbourne and consists of a long, broad street, with a branch from the centre leading to Wycombe. It has a fine church, with many brasses and memorials of the Drakes of Shardeloes, one of whom built the brick town hall, and another the picturesque almshouses, set round a tiny court, in the main street. The new Amersham has arisen on the level ground near the station and is spreading fast in all directions. One of the latest estates to be developed is the Weller Estate, closely adjoining the station.' The estate mentioned was being developed by a subsidiary of the railway company. It covered eighty acres of farmland to the east of the new station, which had been bought up by the Weller family, owners of the Amersham brewery (until bought out by Benskins in 1929), and sold in 1930 to Metropolitan Railway Country Estates Limited, for development in conjunction with the Railway, eventually totalling over 500 houses and fifty shops.

Just before the Second World War, a travellers' guide described Amersham as 'an unusually good example of an old country town. The long wide High Street has quite a remarkable array of sixteenth- and seventeenth-century inns, houses and cottages. These and the old market house and the middle row [the latter about to be demolished as an 'improvement'] and the fine old church, present a store of interest for the visitor and a wealth of subjects for the camera and sketchbook.'

Middle Row has long gone, but the rest still holds true as modern developments have been confined to the eastern edge of the town, where the cottages of Bury End gave way, firstly to Brazil's meat processing factory, replaced later by the even more inappropriate buildings of a Tesco superstore and its accompanying petrol station and car park.

The dates given for the pictures are, except for specific occasions, estimates, mostly accurate to within five years.

one

River Misbourne

In the four miles from its source, the River Misbourne passes through Great and Little Missenden where, in earlier days, it powered two watermills before entering Amersham. A typical chalk stream, or winterbourne, it sometimes disappears underground for long stretches, but in this 1925 photograph it is flowing strongly as it enters Shardeloes Park.

In Shardeloes Park, the Misbourne was dammed in about 1720 to create an ornamental lake covering some thirty acres, including the probable site of a Roman villa. Public footpaths cross the park beside the lake and in the early 1900s camping was allowed there. The squire later withdrew the privilege due to the damage that resulted. Skating was also very popular when the lake, pictured here in 1904, was frozen.

Shardeloes Lake is a haven for many kinds of waterfowl, with some preferring the open waters of the upper end, others the tree-shrouded lower part of the lake. In this 1925 photograph, a solitary swan glides through the still water toward the small wooded island.

Another early twentieth-century photograph of the lake shows the mature trees which surround its lower end. Shardeloes Lake was an angler's paradise, which, between the world wars, yielded the largest pike caught in English waters.

Left: Below the lake, the river is crossed by the Missenden Road bridge, pictured here in about 1925, with Shardeloes Park on the far side of the road, as the river enters Amersham town. The original turnpike road through the park was diverted around the lake when it was created 200 years earlier.

Below: At the western end of Amersham High Street, the ancient Town Mill was powered by the Misbourne, and this 1900 postcard view shows the mill (left) and miller's house, seen across the mill-pond. Built in the early seventeenth century as a corn-mill, it was converted to paper-making 150 years later, but reverted to grinding meal until the Second World War, when the wheel was scrapped for salvage.

THE OLD MILL, AMERSHAM.

Above: Looking at the other side of Town Mill, the tail-race emerges under Mill Lane, where a horse-drawn wagon stands against the mill's loading door, pictured in about 1930 from the footpath to Barn Meadow. From here the river flows behind the properties on the north side of High Street, crossed by several private plank bridges giving the residents direct access to the meadow from their back gates.

Right: Photographed in the winter of 1927 from the back garden of Baker's bakery in High Street, this was the view over the river to Barn Meadow and part of the brewery's nineteenth-century maltings complex. In the background, beyond the snow-covered meadow, are the first houses in School Lane, with Rectory Wood at the crest of the hill.

Left: From the meadow, the Misbourne flows under the brewery's stables and cart sheds, then under Church Street, to emerge between St Mary's church and the brewery, which is behind the high brick wall seen to the right of the stream. Pictured here in about 1925, the placid surface of the water gives a good reflection of the church tower, but in past centuries when the flow was generally much greater, the church was occasionally subject to flooding.

Below: Looking downstream from below the church in 1920, the river flows past the cemetery (behind the brick wall), which was opened in the late nineteenth century when the churchyard became full. The field beside the willow trees, actually an island between two branches of the river, was later used for allotments. The distant house, beyond the line of willows, was associated with the adjacent gasworks.

At the eastern end of Amersham, Station Road was built after the opening of the railway to link the old town to the new, and this bridge, pictured in about 1900, carried the new road over the Misbourne where the river widened into the mill-pond of Bury Mill.

THE MILL STREAM, AMERSHAM.

After Bury Mill, which, by 1931 when this postcard was published, had become the Mill Stream Restaurant, the Misbourne flows under the London Road, emerging beneath the brick parapet to continue through another mill in the open fields between Amersham and Chalfont St Giles, on its way to join the River Colne near Denham.

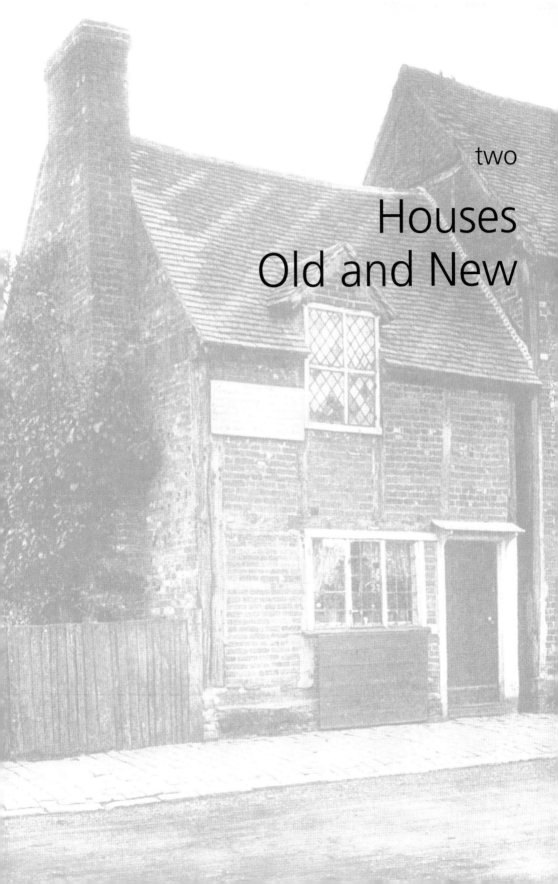

two

Houses
Old and New

Pictured in about 1910, Shardeloes was home to generations of the Tyrwhitt-Drake family, squires of Amersham and owners of most of the town. Racehorses were bred here in the stable block to the right of the house, which was built in 1760, requisitioned for the duration of the Second World War for use as a maternity hospital and in 1958 converted into luxury flats.

Hidden from public view behind its original high brick and flint wall, which closes the westward view along High Street, Little Shardeloes, a fine brick house that was at one time the dower house to Shardeloes mansion, was built in about 1686, with later additions. This postcard view from within the grounds is one of a series published by a local greengrocer in about 1905.

In this 1910 view of the western end of Amersham High Street, the solitary pedestrian is crossing the narrow entrance to Cherry Lane, which then led to the hamlet of Woodrow, but is now blocked by the Amersham bypass. Beyond the turning, partly screened by trees, is The Firs. In the nineteenth century, it was the home of a member of the Weller family, owners of Amersham Brewery. From 1900 it became a doctor's surgery, subsequently renamed Piers Place.

Near the eastern end of Amersham, Broadway House, an Elizabethan residence refronted in the eighteenth century, faces along the street towards the centre of town. Its neighbour to the right, one of a pair of seventeenth-century timber-framed cottages, and once the home of a hunt official, became known as Huntsman's Cottage. Windsor chairs were made in the adjoining cottage, just off the edge of this early 1900s view.

Pictured in 1910, Woodrow High House, built in 1656, was the nucleus of a separate hamlet south of old Amersham and, for a time, the home of Oliver Cromwell's wife and family. It is said to be haunted by the 'Green Lady', the ghost of Lady Helena Stanhope, who committed suicide there after accidentally leading the pursuers of her fiancé Sir Peter Bostock to him during the Civil War.

Amersham Rectory was built on the northern slopes of the Misbourne Valley overlooking Amersham in the seventeenth century. Rebuilt in its present form a century later, the grounds include a timbered well-house where the horse-operated machinery was still in use in the early twentieth century. This picture dates from around 1915, when occasional religious pageants would be held on the lawns in front of the house.

This terrace, Turpins Row, has no connection with the notorious highwayman but belonged to Thomas Turpin in the eighteenth century. Built in about 1607 as four houses, they were later divided into twelve cottages, all different, with back gardens bordering the Misbourne just below Town Mill. In the nineteenth century most of the female residents here were employed making lace or plaiting straw for the Luton hat industry.

The block of tiny whitewashed almshouses near the middle of this view was built at the expense of Andrew Hale, who died in 1697. They were for 'four aged single men or women, selected by the Churchwardens to live there rent-free for life'. When pictured in 1895, the houses were all in poor condition but three were still occupied, however all were demolished four years later.

Above: Still proudly standing in the High Street behind pollarded lime-trees are the Drake Almshouses, built in 1657 by William Drake of Shardeloes for 'six poor widows of farmers and tradesmen'. Pictured in about 1900, they were then described in a county guide as the most charming of all the pretty almshouses in Bucks: 'six little houses with lace curtains at the windows, flowers on the sills and flower-beds in the cobbled yard, all set in its walls like a picture in a frame.'

Left: Almost opposite the Drake Almshouses, and sandwiched between two normal-sized cottages, is the smallest cottage in Amersham, pictured here in 1950. Now known as 'Wee Oaks', it was built in the sixteenth century, then consisting of only two rooms, with the upper one well into the roof space.

Until 1939, a block of cottages continued the line of the old Church House along to the malthouse, where the Memorial Garden now is. A further block, without backyards, stood in front of them, separated only by the narrow Back Alley. The front block, known as Church Row or Middle Row, is pictured here in about 1900. All were demolished to ease traffic flow at the Whielden Street junction immediately before the Second World War.

Whielden Street, which was shown on a map of 1742 as Wilding Street, and which was temporarily renamed Union Street after the opening of the Union Workhouse, is also lined with sixteenth- and seventeenth-century cottages, some divided from larger houses, and a few former shops. Looking back into town with the hill and woods beyond, in about 1930, the first cottage on the left, on the corner of The Platt, had been a Windsor Chair factory, and still retains the former timber-drying sheds at the back, alongside the lane.

Above: The Platt, a narrow lane off Whielden Street, leads behind the long gardens on the south side of High Street, continuing as a footpath as far as Shardeloes Park. In this lane, tucked well away from the busy streets, is the seventeenth-century timber-framed Chimney Cottage, probably the most distinctive of Amersham's many attractive cottages.

AMERSHAM, THE OLD COTTAGE.

Left: This 300-year old cottage at the end of Broadway, still carries a notice, dated 24 June 1811, warning unwanted visitors entering the town that 'The Magistrates acting for this hundred have given peremptory Order to the Constables and other Peace Officers to apprehend all Common Beggars, Ballad Singers and other Vagrants so that they may be dealt with according to the Law'.

Broadway continues east beyond the Gore Hill turning as London Road, through Bury End, at one time a separate community, although less than 100 yards separated it from Amersham. Looking back towards the town in about 1900, the cottages of Bury End face the waterworks across a wide, traffic-free road. These cottages were demolished in the 1940s, replaced initially by Brazil's Sausage factory and now by Tesco's car park.

The original open space of Amersham Common stretched for a couple of miles along the ridge north of the Misbourne valley, from the present-day Amersham on the Hill to Little Chalfont. Round its edge a few farms and cottages were built as early as the seventeenth century. This postcard, published in about 1920, shows a pair of old cottages which stood where the edge of the shopping centre of Amersham on the Hill is now.

Before the coming of the railway, scattered groups of cottages already existed along White Lion Road at the edge of Amersham Common, mostly occupied by workers on the neighbouring farms. The building boom which followed the arrival of the railway filled many of the gaps between the earlier properties, and this early twentieth-century postcard shows a mixture of old and new cottages in the area, which is still known as Amersham Common.

Looking back through the modern Amersham Common towards Amersham town in about 1910, the left (south) side of White Lion Road was already becoming built up, but there were only a couple of properties on the north side, which formed part of the Duke of Bedford's Chenies Estate and where the new railway runs only some 200 yards from the road.

Loudham's Cottages, on the corner of Burtons Lane and the main Amersham to Rickmansworth road were shown on a 1770 map. Still isolated when pictured here in about 1915, despite the arrival of the nearby railway twenty-five years earlier, they were sold in 1920 with the fields of Loudhams Farm, but remained, in the midst of the growing shopping centre, until Little Chalfont Village Green was created on the site in 1967.

After the 1892 opening of the railway, Station Road was constructed through this dry valley linking the new community on the hill with the old town below. Piecemeal housing development started halfway down the hill in about 1910, and this was the scene some five years later, with houses spaced randomly over the slope below Rectory Wood, facing the open fields below Batchelors Wood on the opposite slope.

The country's first 'Modern movement' house, High and Over, was built in 1930 on the crest of the slope above Station Road, with its own water tower. It was joined in 1933 by a group of Sun Houses in similar style beside its curving drive. The group of houses, a focus for architects, upset many locals, one of whom, when asked what he thought of them, replied, 'we don't think of them, we just don't look at them'. This picture was printed soon after their completion, before further building on that slope.

Station Road,   Amersham.

These terraced houses, in Station Road above the railway bridge, were the first of the new town, built before the turn of the century and pictured shortly afterwards looking downhill from the site where the new grammar school would soon be built. A large sign on the bridge points the way to Amersham station.

After the Great War, development started on the western side of Amersham on the Hill, with individually designed luxury houses on extensive sites in Hervines Road. This postcard shows Beaumont, the home of Rear Admiral Edouard Gaudin from 1924 until the early 1930s, with a note on the back of the card that the four-acre plot, with a 500ft frontage, was priced at £800.

CORNER OF LITTLE CHALFONT

This 1926 postcard uses the new name, given only the previous year, to the growing community around Chalfont Road station. In 1922, these first houses were built in Village Way, with roofs thatched as an economy measure, in a hollow beside the railway embankment. Unfortunately sparks from the passing steam engines caused many roof fires, and most were replaced by tiles within a few years.

Right: Wellers, the wealthy Amersham brewing family, sold their extensive lands in 'top' Amersham to Metropolitan Railway Country Estates Ltd, who then developed them, selling either houses completed to one of their standard patterns or plots on which buyers could erect homes to their own design. This advertisement appeared in the railway's *Metroland* guide in 1932.

Below: Development of the Weller Estate started in the early 1930s with Woodside Close, next to the new town shops, then in The Rise, The Green and The Drive immediately south of the railway. Later that decade, the builders moved north to Woodside Road, Highfield Close, and Grimsdells Lane, but work here was delayed by the war. This photograph from 1985 is the only known picture to show the typical Metroland houses of Highfield Close.

These three corrugated iron dwellings were built in about 1920 in a close off White Lion Road near the Pineapple Inn. Known as Bendrose Bungalows, they were built on the edge of Bendrose Farm's land to house local workers, and remained in use for over forty years until replaced by conventional houses.

Amersham's first council housing was built in the early 1920s and consisted of eight pairs of semi-detached houses on a two-acre field between White Lion Road and the railway line next to Bell Lane. This view across White Lion Road and down Bell Lane to the railway bridge was published in about 1925.

three

Refreshment

The tiny hamlet of Mop End, just off the Wycombe Road near the top of Shardeloes Park, consisted of a farm, a few cottages and a pub, the Old Griffin, bought by Wellers brewery in 1775. When pictured, in 1915, George Wilkins had already been landlord for ten years, and he remained there, doubling as chair manufacturer, until after the Second World War. Over a mile from any other community, there were few regulars, apart from the graziers on nearby Wycombe Heath, and the bodgers delivering chair parts for assembly here.

Opposite above: In this 1903 view, The Hare & Hounds faces The Nag's Head across the town end of Whielden Street. Built in about 1700, The Hare & Hounds was a small cottage, sandwiched between a greengrocer's shop and a further terrace of cottages. Charles Arnott was a bootmaker as well as landlord of the larger, detached, Nag's Head at this time, where the side wall, facing into town, was used as an advertisement hoarding.

Opposite below: Toward the western end of High Street, The Swan was one of Amersham's several coaching inns. The inn and the adjoining house are both seventeenth-century timber-framed buildings but the inn was later given a more fashionable brick front. The house still displays its timber construction.

This 1915 view of the western half of High Street, which has been described as 'an exhibition of the architecture of the last 500 years' and 'the most attractive street in Buckinghamshire', includes the gabled Elephant & Castle. Another timber-framed early seventeenth-century building, it hides its framework behind modern rough-cast. The next-door shop was the birthplace of Brazil's pie and sausage business.

On the left of this 1905 view, The Red Lion, opened by Wellers in 1837, catered specially for cyclists; it was advertised as a 'cyclist's rest' as well as repairing and hiring machines. It closed after exactly 100 years. Across the road, another Weller house, The King's Arms, is hardly recognisable as the popular inn of today, its brick and timber construction being hidden by an early nineteenth-century frontage.

This picture of the back of The King's Arms, also from 1905, reveals some of the original sixteenth-century construction, although the arch had been enlarged 200 years later for the large coaches which then required access to the yard in order to change horses.

The annexe to the right of The King's Arms is even older than the main building, and is considered to be one of the best examples of fifteenth-century building work. In 1936 it was incorporated with the hotel, which was re-fronted again to match the genuine timbering of the annexe.

In Market Square The Crown, another coaching inn, hides its 400-year old timbered front behind brickwork added 200 years later, when it also housed the local Inland Revenue office and the petty sessional court. A feature of this 1910 view of The Crown is the portico over the main door. Supported on wooden pillars, it extended to the kerb, but was removed in the 1960s after several mishaps with passing vehicles. The off-licence is to the right of the carriage arch, with Metropolitan Railway timetables displayed outside.

The back of The Crown is seen here in about 1925, when it was advertised as 'a picturesque old house with all modern comforts'. A few years later a guide writer noted that the vine on the coffee-house wall bore heavy crops of black grapes. The large gateway to the street, still with its original timbers, allowed access for the many carriages which entered the cobbled yard.

"THE WILLOW TREE", OLD AMERSHAM

A typical English tea room, The Willow Tree Café occupied part of the old grammar school building next to the churchyard from the 1940s until the '80s. In the exterior picture, the café's signboard in its little side garden is almost hidden by the tree which gave it its name. Access was by a new doorway next to the old school entrance under its stone arch, inscribed 'grammar school 1624' . The welcoming interior, with various styles of Windsor chair at polished wooden tables under a beamed ceiling, was enhanced by vases of real flowers on the tables. The homely atmosphere, which earned it the accolade 'restaurant of the year' awarded by the Family Welcome guide, gave the ideal setting for the home-cooked food served at morning coffee, luncheon and afternoon tea. Both pictures were published as postcards for sale in the café in the 1950s.

THE WILLOW TREE

16TH CENTURY

OLD AMERSHAM

Left: The Griffin Hotel, when photographed in about 1895, still carried a hanging sign offering Post Horses, beside the picture of the mythical Griffin. The tallest building in Amersham, which enjoyed renown as a coaching inn, it was rebuilt in the seventeenth century, but the stables and other outbuildings accommodating the coach drivers and postillions are original. Much later, the cobbled yard was to witness a very different form of transport as the base for the Amersham & District Bus Company.

Below: Pictured in 1935 with a disguised electricity substation outside, Ye Olde Malt Tea House opened in Broadway in the early 1930s, with advertisements stating 'From 1425 to 1907 this perfect oak-beamed and timbered building was used for brewing beer, now it is a delightful tea house with accommodation for eighty persons'. Visitors were welcomed by the wooden cut-out of a crinolined lady outside the front door.

The tea house and its gardens extended some way back from the road toward the river. Part of the rear of the building had been severely damaged by fire in 1884, but it was carefully restored and some of the original wattle and daub walling was displayed behind a glass panel in the tea room. A local solicitor had bought the building when disused after 1907 in order to preserve 'this Tudor gem'.

INTERIOR
YE OLDE MALTE TEA HOUSE, AMERSHAM.

Another postcard dating from the same time as the previous two, this shows a part of the inside with a selection of old and contemporary items on display on the mantelshelf of the brick fireplace built within the original open hearth chimney. Fine views over the river to Rectory Hill were seen from the large timbered upstairs room of the restaurant, which boasted that everything served was home-made.

No longer working, Bury Mill, over 400 years old, was part of the Shardeloes estate sold off in 1928. Three years later it opened as a roadhouse, soon becoming the high-class Mill Stream restaurant. The proprietors later added an antique business in the small annexe near the road. When the old mill was converted to a restaurant, the gallery was added overlooking the newly installed dance floor, and a feature was made of the river flowing through the middle of the building, visible through a plate glass panel. On New Year's Eve 1956 a Carnival Dinner Dance cost two guineas a head, and diners were advised that 'the ghost that haunts the old mill' would appear at midnight.

Next door to The Mill Stream and sharing the same forecourt is another old inn, The Chequers. Built of brick and flint in the seventeenth century, and re-fronted when bought by the Amersham brewery in 1802, it still advertised their brew when pictured here in the 1930s although Wellers had sold up in 1929. As was common at the time, an early Victorian landlord here had a second occupation, in this case as a butter dealer, able to use the cellar for cool storage.

Above: Quick to tap a new source of custom, Wellers built The Station Hotel in 1893, facing the newly opened Amersham station, transferring the licence from The Black Horse at Amersham Common, which had closed due to the construction of the railway. Some two years later, landlord Arthur Muckley advertised 'billiards, tennis, excellent stabling, and every accommodation for bean feasts and parties of up to fifty'.

Left: The Metropolitan Temperance Hotel in Station Road also opened immediately after the railway brought potential customers. Run in conjunction with the adjoining confectionery shop and sub post office, when pictured in 1910 it was under 'the personal supervision of the proprietress, Mrs Laura Nevell'.

The Boot & Slipper

MR. & MRS. A.W. SMITH
(BERT & MURIEL)

AMERSHAM,

BUCKS.

FULLY LICENSED

TEL: AMERSHAM 1082.

The Boot & Slipper, which dates back to 1611, stood almost alone on the edge of Amersham Common, serving mainly those who farmed the common and the occupants of a couple of nearby cottages in Rickmansworth Road, until the rapid twentieth-century development of Amersham on the Hill all around it. Wellers had added it to their growing number of tied houses in 1849. This multi-view postcard was published by the landlord in about 1960.

The brick and flint Black Horse, the origin of the name by which the nearby railway bridge is still known, closed when the railway was built on an embankment only a few feet from its front door. Its licence was then transferred by Wellers to their new Station Hotel. This picture was taken by a Chesham photographer in winter shortly before its closure. Landlord George Line was also a wheelwright, and he continued that business next to the old town's gasworks after the pub's closure.

Opposite above: The Bijou Tea Table opened in The Beeches, a narrow detached house in White Lion Road about 100 yards from Black Horse bridge, from 1910 to 1930. It catered primarily for the walkers and cyclists who sought the rural atmosphere, open views and fresh air of the Chiltern countryside. For cyclists, it provided a tyre repair service, probably very necessary given the state of the road surfaces.

Opposite below: The Pineapple Inn, first licensed in 1830, but in a much older building set back from the road, was actually at the edge of the common land onto which its neighbours had encroached as far as the unfenced Amersham to Rickmansworth road. The inn, which served the local farm workers, is believed to take its name from the crest of the Pomeroy family, owners of West Indian fruit plantations, who lived in nearby Beel House.

The BIJOU
TEA ROOMS

CHESHAM GOLD MEDAL ALES

THE PINEAPPLE
AMERSHAM COMMON

THE WHITE LION, AMERSHAM COMMON.

The White Lion stands on the corner of the Amersham to Rickmansworth road and Finch Lane, which was once a main link to the Misbourne Valley. Shown on an 1820 county map, it gave the name to this section of the main road and catered for travellers along that road. The single-storey front part of the inn had probably been added in 1888 to accommodate the navvies then working locally on the Metropolitan Railway.

four

Places
of Learning

THE OLD GRAMMAR SCHOOL, AMERSHAM.

In 1905, Doctor Challoner's grammar school moved to a new building on a six-acre site provided by the Drake family in the new town near the top of Rectory Hill. It was partly financed by the Local Education Authority on condition that it became co-educational. The new school, which accommodated 100 pupils, is pictured here in 1910 with the integral headmaster's house at the right-hand end. Subsequent expansion surrounded this original building with overbearing modern additions, and eventually necessitated growth on to a second site. The girls then transferred to the new Doctor Challoner's High School at Little Chalfont and the grammar school was once again for boys only.

Opposite above: Amersham's Free Grammar School for Boys was established in 1624 under the will of Doctor Robert Chaloner, rector of Amersham from 1576, who died in 1621. At first it occupied the former Church House, the creeper-clad end of the block facing Market Square in this 1945 view. Before this, Church House had at one time served as the Parish Room, and had also been used as the parish workhouse.

Opposite below: In the eighteenth century, the number of pupils fell seriously, the grammar school was temporarily housed in the Market Hall and the Church House was then used by a rival establishment, Lord Cheyne's Writing School. Then in 1736 the grammar school master, with some of the pupils as boarders, moved into this newly rebuilt house in the High Street, and teaching took place next door.

These pictures of the new grammar school, from its prospectus of about 1915, show two classrooms opened up as one large room (above), and the laboratory (below). The prospectus makes much of the healthy, bracing air of the district, which is due to its altitude. The headmaster and his wife also cared for a limited number of boarders and provided hot dinners for day pupils, quoting the following fees per term: dinners £1 10s, boarding £12, tuition £3.

Better known as the offices of the district council from 1931 to 1986, after it was renamed Elmodesham House, the large square building toward the left of this 1925 view had once been a flourishing private school. Built in 1705 for a wealthy merchant and then named Woodville House, Ebenezer West set up his 'Academy for the Sons of Liberal Gentlemen' there in 1829, but moved it away in 1861, as the lack of a railway hindered his expansion plans.

Amersham National School was built in 1873 on a site given by the rector in Wych Field, alongside Back Lane. Originally built for 300 pupils, it needed extension before the end of the century. Pictured from Barn Meadow in the 1900s, the school was by then known as St Mary's and the road as School Lane.

The oldest parts of St Mary's church were built in the thirteenth and fourteenth centuries. The tower was added in the fifteenth, when the floor level was raised over three feet to above the flood level of the adjacent river, and the roof was also raised. This drawing dates from around 1850, when a guide noted simply that the church is 'near the middle of the town, built of brick, covered with stucco'.

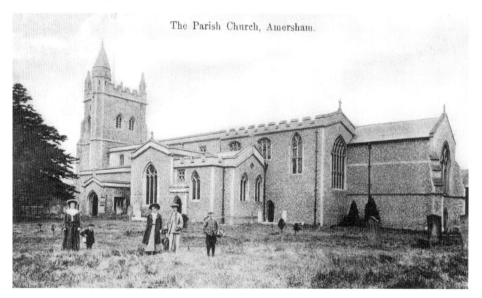

The Parish Church, Amersham.

The church's exterior was restored in 1889, partly funded by the Drake family, when the walls were refaced with flints dug while excavating a cutting for the new railway line between Amersham and Great Missenden. The top of the tower was also remodelled with four pinnacles, the largest of which contains the top of the tower staircase, giving access to the roof.

Above: This 1900 photograph of the south porch of the church shows the detail of the knapped flint facing with stone dressings. The solidity of its construction suggests that the porch was originally intended to have an upper storey. The Victorian restoration removed the sundial from above the entrance arch, but the iron gates inside the entrance were left in place.

Right: Among the features of the chancel on this 1915 postcard are some of the original grotesque creatures carved on the stone corbels supporting the vaulted wooden ceiling, and the east window containing seventeenth-century stained glass given by the Drake family. Behind the high altar is a three-section Victorian carved reredos, now hidden since the architect of the 1965 interior restoration considered it commonplace. On the walls are some of the monuments for which the church is renowned.

AMERSHAM CHURCH.

59453.

Above: In 1907 St Mary's established a mission church to serve the growing population of Amersham Common, in a pair of former railway contractors' cottages, rebuilt on White Lion Road opposite Black Horse Bridge. The brick and corrugated iron building is pictured in 1910 with the National School, now known as St George's, behind and to its left.

Left: Pictured at about the same date, the neatly laid out interior of the church contrasts with its utilitarian exterior. This second-hand building remained in service for twenty-eight years until the construction of the permanent church half a mile along the road toward Little Chalfont.

St George's, the permanent church for Amersham Common and Little Chalfont, was built further along White Lion Road in 1935, replacing the temporary 'tin church' at the other end of Amersham Common. It was designed to be extended later when funds permitted, but this has not yet happened. Access was initially over the roadside ditch via a simple footbridge, visible outside the gate pillars on the left of this photograph taken shortly after the opening.

In 1689, part of Joseph Winch's cottage in Whielden Street was registered as a Meeting House for local Quakers who then numbered about 100. After 1750 their numbers steadily dwindled and the meetings ceased in 1853. The building was then leased to the Methodists who had no chapel of their own until 1899. Pictured across the road in 1915, it remained unused until 1917 when regular Quaker meetings were revived.

Amersham Free Church stood next door to St Michael's Hall in Sycamore Road. The Free Church, nearer the camera on this 1955 photograph, had been built before the First World War. Beyond it, the 1927 'temporary' church hall of St Mary's mission church (St Michael's) stood in front of another 'temporary' structure, built in 1920 as the church but designed to become the hall when they could afford a permanent church.

Built in 1911 and extended four years later to seat 450, the interior of the Free Church is pictured here in 1958. A comment on the back of the postcard noted that all was in light oak with a blue carpet and lights, also that the organ, above the choir on the left, was too much sometimes.

Right: The large plot occupied by the two churches was a prime site in the middle of the main shopping centre and the 1961 sale of most of it for development raised enough money for both churches to be rebuilt. The Free Church then moved to Sycamore Corner, but the new St Michael's church was built in front of the 1920 hall, and was dedicated in 1966. This photograph shows the back of the new church under construction and the corner of the old hall.

Below: Local Methodists first met in a cottage in Bury End in 1818. Then from 1851, they rented the disused Friends' Meeting House. In 1899 the permanent Methodist chapel was built on the site of Lane's almshouses in the High Street opposite The Swan. Described as 'a compact red brick church, set behind a line of spiked iron railings', it is pictured in 1910.

Left: Amersham's memorial to those who died in the 1914–18 war was unveiled in the churchyard in July 1921. Despite its proximity to the corner of the chancel, the 1925 photographer managed to exclude the church, just out of view to the left of the narrow path. The conical structure behind the memorial is the roof of a stream-side summer-house in the garden beyond the brewery.

Below: When the Garden of Remembrance was laid out after the Second World War, the First World War Memorial Cross was moved to a prominent position in it, with the beautiful background of trees capped by Rectory Wood. The garden with its central pond, well-maintained flower beds and neatly manicured areas of grass was photographed shortly after completion from an upstairs window of The Griffin Hotel across the road.

five

Shopping

Market Square, Amersham

William Broadwater was the mid-nineteenth-century owner of this chemist's shop in Market Square where he printed and issued a broadsheet of local news, primarily to advertise his many-sided business as 'printer, bookseller, stationer, book-binder, artificial manure merchant, oil and colourman, circulating library, and newsagent, chemist and druggist'. After several changes of ownership, Amersham's first local newspaper survives today as the *Buckinghamshire Advertiser*. In 1865 the business was bought by Thomas King who, with son Ebenezer, also shared the duties of local registrar of births and deaths toward the end of the century. Ebenezer took over the business in about 1900, when this picture was taken, followed by Mrs Jane King between the wars, and it remained in the family until the 1960s.

Above: In the narrow part of the street opposite Middle Row was Mead's grocery stores, which opened here in the 1870s in the bay-windowed front rooms of the original cottage. Pictured here in 1910, the smartly dressed owner stands in the doorway and his assistant by their rebuilt shop front, while the shop lad is checking boxes, including one of Crawford's biscuits, on a laden cart in the side passageway.

Right: Arthur Bailey owned the first antique shop in Amersham High Street. His signboard gives an establishment date of 1852, which was when Thomas Bailey started business as a carpenter. Around the turn of the century, Arthur took over, becoming an antique furniture dealer before the Great War. This 1920 view of the shop front includes members of the Bailey family who continued the business until its centenary, under Mrs Annie Bailey from the early 1920s, followed by Miss Rosina Bailey in the late '30s.

Fuller's drapery was established by Henry Fuller in this seventeenth-century building in Whielden Street, which had been the workhouse, just after the inmates moved out in 1889. Frederick Fuller continued the business from 1924 until 1950, with a second shop in Hill Avenue in the 1930s. This 1910 view shows that it stocked much more than just drapery, resulting in its local nickname 'The Emporium'.

Ernest Wilson's hairdressing salon and tobacco shop stood on this corner from the beginning of the twentieth century, with its display window, including a selection of postcards, facing Market Square and its entrance around the corner in Church Street. The view into Church Street is one of Amersham's most popular subjects for artists and photographers, and this postcard, published in 1915, is just one of nearly a hundred similar views.

Right: Facing the corner of Whielden Street, John Whiteside's bakery, pictured in 1910, occupied one of the cottages of Middle Row from 1900 until shortly before the block was demolished. His bakehouse extended into the cottage behind, and the loaves had to be carried across Back Alley to the shop. Much of the bread was delivered by horse-drawn van as far as the new town up the hill.

Below: George Ward, Amersham's most prolific photographer in the late nineteenth and early twentieth centuries, also managed the gasworks in the 1880s. He started an ironmongery business at the turn of the century in the three-gabled building on the right of this 1950 view. In the early 1920s he also manufactured cycles at 'The Wizard Works' there, adding motor engineering a year or two later.

MARKET PLACE AND CROWN HOTEL, OLD AMERSHAM

Above: Hill's Stores was established by George William Hill in about 1905. It was taken over by Kinghams, the small chain of high-class grocery shops in about 1930, but continued trading under the original name, as seen on this 1940 photograph, until the early 1960s.

Left: Throughout the 1930s, Climpson & Sons' boot and shoe shop stood in the High Street, just west of the Market Hall, beside the entrance to the narrow path along its north side. Besides making and repairing footwear, they were also clothiers and sellers of leather and grindery, with a variety of goods displayed in the windows.

The Broadway, Amersham.

Above: In 1910 it was safe to stop for a chat in the middle of the road at the foot of Whielden Street, in front of Whiteside's bakery. Joyce's shop had first opened on the corner about five years earlier, selling oils, paints and general furnishings, some displayed outside, and also ammunition. In 1923 Frederick Gascoyne, previously another of Amersham's cycle makers, took over the business, continuing until the Second World War.

Right: Tom Llewellyn Baker, baker by trade as well as name, lived behind his bakery in the High Street which was open from 1912 until 1950. In this 1928 photo he is standing outside the door of his shop accompanied by one of his daughters. As with all their neighbours, their back garden ended at the river bank and they had a simple plank bridge across the water to Barn Meadow.

The first shops of the new town were built in Station Road just below the railway bridge from which this 1913 photograph was taken. The single shop on the right, named Osborne House, opened in 1907 as Toovey's furniture shop, followed in 1912 by William Mead's drapery, a business continued by Renshaw & Sons from 1924 until the 1980s. On the other side of the road Station Parade had been developed by estate agent W.J. Sumner, who later opened one of its shops as Sumner's Domestic Stores, boasting 'everything for the home at London prices'. The corner shop in the parade was London House, a drapery and outfitting business run by the Misses Peck, who also published many postcards of Amersham.

These shops at Oakfield Corner, with Arthur Kennard's chemists shop in the prime position, were designed by Arthur's architect brother John, who also designed many Amersham houses before the First World War. These shops were built in two phases, the corner block in 1912 followed by blocks in both Chesham Road and Sycamore Road a year later, starting the main shopping centre of Amersham on the Hill. This postcard view was published in 1915 when Harry Plummer's greengrocery occupied the Sycamore Road shop under the wide glass veranda.

Looking back to Oakfield Corner from Chesham Road in 1930, a thick hedge separates the corner shops from the next block, in which sun blinds protect the windows of 'The Old Dairy' and Berkeley's butchers shop. On the far side of the crossroads the single-storey Barclays Bank and Coles' Bucks County Library adjoin the first buildings of Hill Avenue.

Estate agents Pretty & Ellis started business in Amersham just after the First World War in this wooden building in Station Approach, backing onto the station's up platform. They were closely involved in much of the growth of Amersham on the Hill as architects, surveyors and property developers. Pictured in 1930, they moved shortly afterwards to new offices just up the road in Hill Avenue.

Although the railway opened in 1892, Hill Avenue, the direct link between the station and the new town, did not even exist until 1910, and then remained unsurfaced until the late 1920s. This 1924 postcard shows, on the right, the well-separated shops near the station and the newly built block nearer the top of the hill with a couple of private houses on the left of the rough road.

A few years later and most of the gaps on the right-hand side had been filled with new buildings, including Station Garages two doors from the corner. Further up the road Pope's corn and seed merchants were 'sole agents for Featheration complete laying meal' and Stacey's butchers advertised 'high-class pork and beef purveyors; hams, tongues and table delicacies always in stock; families waited on and supplied promptly'.

THE CREAMERIES
J. B. WHITING, Proprietor.

Dairyman

"GRADE A"
T.T.
MILK

Cream, Butter
Eggs, Honey.

BROCKLEY
Pork Pies and
Sausages.

**All foods fresh
from local farms
daily.**

Telephone:
Amersham 235.

THE HYGIENIC CREAMERIES, Hill Avenue, Amersham-on-the-Hill.

This Hill Avenue dairy seems to have had unusually frequent changes of management. In 1926, proprietor G. Ayres advertised their specialities: 'nursery milk in sealed bottles for infants and invalids', and clotted cream. Two years later Albert Richards was in charge, followed by Richard Gamble, then by J.B. Whiting, whose illustrated advertisement in the 1933 town guide is pictured here.

The top end of Hill Avenue is seen here in 1940 looking over the forecourt of the National Provincial Bank, whose modern corner building replaced their temporary home on the opposite corner. At the left edge is the 1936 shop of the Chesham & Wycombe Co-Operative Society, next to Kathleen Graham's restaurant and confectioners shop and Spencer's tobacconists. Behind the fir tree was the last remaining private house on that side of the road.

OAKFIELD CORNER, AMERSHAM-ON-THE-HILL

Above: Postmarked 1936, this view shows the partly-completed shopping centre of Sycamore Road, where the shops on the right included: Howards Estate Agents, Bucks County Library, Barclays, Lloyds and Westminster Banks, Kennards Chemists, Jane Evans hats and gowns and an empty plot on the corner of Woodside Close. The next block included Napiers drapery (Woodcocks) and Brownings hardware store.

Right: Pisces, who advertised as 'high-class fishmongers, poulterers, licensed game dealers and ice merchants', occupied premises in Sycamore Road from 1924 to 1929 and this photograph shows their filleting bench at the back of the shop. At that time they were in competition with six other local fishmongers, three in the new town and two in the old, plus another in White Lion Road.

A pair of shops stood in isolation further along Sycamore Road in 1925. Winifred Williams, milliner and children's outfitter, occupied Burlington House, the further shop, while the other was Tunstall's Sycamore Library, 'an up-to-date lending library in connection with Harrods, sole agent for the celebrated Tulip wool, also bookseller, tobacconist and fancy goods'.

This was the view in 1930 looking back along Sycamore Road from outside the Regent Cinema. Two private houses, Ashcot and Romney Cottage, remained in their large gardens between Regent Buildings adjoining the cinema and the shops nearer Oakfield Corner, until bought for Sainsbury's development of Chiltern Parade, which completed the line of shops.

This photograph of the further part of Sycamore Road dates from 1937, when Chiltern Parade was under construction (at the left edge). Beyond it, Regent Buildings and the cinema had been built in 1928, and they are followed by a further parade extending to Sycamore Corner. To the right of the trees, the sheds of Hall's Hollybush Nursery were due to disappear a couple of years later, to make way for Woolworths.

Published in 1950, this view of Sycamore Road includes the completed Chiltern Parade, where Sainsburys, in the taller central position, was flanked by Freeman Hardy & Willis, Meyers greengrocers, Beckleys radio shop, and Boots. Behind the trees, St Michael's Church Hall occupied part of the site which was to prove a gold-mine for the church in the 1960s.

The first shops in White Lion Road opened before 1900 in some of the old cottages which lined the edge of the original Amersham Common. Sarah Anne Clark's general store is at the right edge of this 1908 view with an enamel sign for R. White's lemonade and ginger beer on the garden fence of the neighbouring house, where a small drapery business was set up in the front parlour. Other shops were scattered at intervals along the road, including Emily Pasmore's grocery shop and sub post office in the building at the other edge of the picture.

Opposite above: The new steeply-roofed building prominent in this late 1920s view along White Lion Road housed Clark's bakery and Goodred's butchers shop. The little wooden building this side of them and next to the Amersham Common Recreation Hall was Bizzell's grocery stores. The railway runs behind these shops on an embankment, part of which can be seen over the road in the distance.

Opposite below: Little Chalfont's first shops, built in 1925, are at the right edge of this late 1940s view. Beyond them the Sugar Loaves public house, set back out of sight, and the parade of shops and garage all date from the early 1930s, and the telephone exchange at the far end from 1937. The wooden hut by the bus stop and pub sign housed a part-time branch of Barclays Bank.

AMERSHAM COMMON. FWM 1788.

Little Chalfont, Station Road.

LC.1

Building at Nightingale Corner, to the right in the upper 1965 view, started in 1929 with Berkeley's butchers and its neighbours, Cullens the grocers. More building, a few years later, extended the parade to the right into Cokes Lane, seen on the lower 1950 postcard, including the Nightingale Café, with its pictorial sign out on the pavement. The further block in the top picture, Chenies Parade, was a 1962 development which still left Loudhams Cottages undisturbed on the corner between the shops.

six

Industry

Chairmaking in Buckinghamshire Woods.

The manufacture of Windsor chairs, which later became the main industry in southern Bucks, started in the eighteenth century as a local craft, based on the bodgers who produced the legs, stretchers and back spindles, using pole lathes in primitive shelters among their raw material, the abundant beech trees of the Chilterns. The bodgers, pictured here in 1900, were already being replaced by urban factories, and became extinct by 1960.

Windsor chair seats were hewn from solid planks and the chairs were then assembled in small workshops, often run as a sideline to other businesses as at the Old Griffin, Mop End, where the landlord doubled as chairmaker. This postcard view of the pub, with piles of seat blanks being seasoned in front, dates from 1920, when there were still six other chairmakers also working in Amersham.

In Queen Victoria's reign, the first small chair factories were set up in the towns and villages around High Wycombe, bringing all the processes together on one site, as in Joseph Hatch & Sons' factory alongside Whielden Lane between Amersham and Winchmore Hill, pictured in 1912. Most of the finished chairs were taken by horse-cart for sale at Windsor market, which gave them their name.

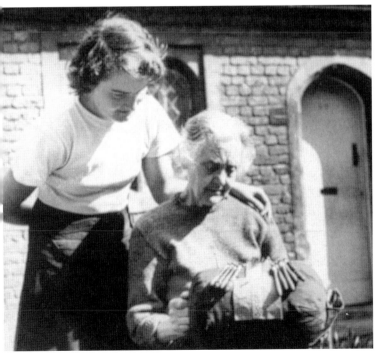

A true 'cottage' industry, which employed many local women in the eighteenth century, was the making of pillow lace, and Amersham market was an important centre for its sale. Competition from machines in the nineteenth century generally reduced the demand for the hand-made product, though Amersham lace was still wanted because of its exceptional quality, but even that later died out commercially. It continued only as a hobby, and in this 1960 photograph one of the residents of the Drake almshouses is making lace in the courtyard.

St. Mary's, Amersham.

The brewery, which was already well over 100 years old when the Weller family bought it in 1775, became Amersham's largest employer. During the following century it bought up many pubs in the local area which then sold Weller's Entire, their most popular brew. This postcard, published in 1905, shows part of the brewery beside the parish church, separated only by the Misbourne.

The brewery's maltings in Barn Meadow, behind the houses of High Street, are at the lower left of this 1920 aerial photo. To the left of the church is the actual brewery, with the stables and dray yard in front, between Church Street and the meadow known as Pondwicks. The brewery closed after its 1929 sale to Benskins, and the maltings became a fabric printing works.

Goya Limited, the perfume manufacturers, moved to Buckingham when they were bombed out of their London factory in 1940. Then in 1946, they took over the old brewery buildings as factory and offices, using this wing as their laboratory. They remained in Amersham, opening a second factory in the new town, until 1984 when the whole operation moved to Derbyshire.

Built early in the sixteenth century, Bury Mill, at the eastern end of Amersham, was always a corn mill, which was part of the Drake's Shardeloes Estate until sold off in 1928. Seen here across the mill-pond in 1900, it had then stopped working due to the restricted flow of the Misbourne following the construction of the Station Road bridge, just upstream, a few years earlier.

Boughton's agricultural engineering and artesian well-boring business started in Chenies in 1897, but moved in 1906 to a site in Bell Lane, beside the railway line. This photograph of their works dates from 1915, when they advertised themselves as 'Agricultural implement makers, steam road roller owners, steam haulage and threshing contractors'. In the 1930s, their heavy equipment was much in demand for building airfields.

Opposite above: The Amersham Gas Light and Coke Company was established in 1854 and the gasworks, with a single gas-holder near the river, was soon feeding thirteen street lamps in the High Street. Although the first gas-holder was well hidden from view, a later addition was much more obvious, particularly when full, and though most photographers managed to exclude it, nothing could hide it completely, as this 1983 Broadway view demonstrates.

Opposite below: The National Benzole Company opened an oil depot adjoining Chalfont and Latimer station in the early 1930s with storage tanks on what is now the lower station car park, remaining there until about 1960. The fuel was brought in by special trains, unloaded from extra sidings alongside the bay used by the Chesham shuttle train. This 1947 view of the station includes a siding full of tank wagons.

Amersham International, the town's largest employer at the end of the twentieth century, started in a small way in 1940 on a site adjacent to the White Lion pub. Here, as Thorium Limited, they refined radium to make the luminous paint needed for aircraft instruments. After the war, renamed The Radiochemical Centre, they were leaders in the development of radioactive materials for medical research and treatment. This postcard shows the front of the site in 1950.

Although the building of new Amersham was planned by large property developers, local builders, some of whom became developers in their own small way, did much of the actual work, including specialised buildings such as schools, churches and the cinema. This team of local workers built St Michael's church hall in 1920.

The main industry in Amersham was originally farming, mostly on small farms rented from the Drake family who owned most of the town and surrounding land. Mantles Green Farm, pictured here in 1930, a cattle farm on both sides of School Lane, near the gates of Shardeloes, became the venue for the traditional Boxing Day meet after increased traffic drove it from Market Square.

Town Farm is almost in the centre of town, next to the Drake Almshouses. From there, Alfred Hoare started supplying the old town with milk in about 1910 and Town Farm Dairy was still the only one in the town until the 1930s. Milk was delivered to Amersham residents from a highly polished churn carried, together with the necessary measuring jugs, on the three-wheeled cart pictured in the High Street in the 1920s.

Amersham looking North.

This 1905 picture of Amersham was taken from the fields of Crown Farm, when the corn had been cut and was awaiting collection. The view, from the slope of Coleshill Down, includes the heart of the town in the valley, with Rectory Wood, to the right of The Rectory, hiding the new town which was beginning to grow on the hilltop.

Opposite above: Pictured in the mid-1920s, these are the barns of Crown Farm behind the farmhouse in Whielden Street. Known as Child's Farm when the Drake family bought it early in the nineteenth century, it became Crown Farm when a later lessee was also tenant of the Crown Inn. When the Amersham and District Bus Company started operating, the farmyard gave them access to an old track leading to the yard of the Griffin Hotel.

Opposite below: Several small farms were spread on the hillside near Amersham Common. One of these was Moody's Farm, named after its 1815 occupant. This postcard view of the old farmhouse, which was later renamed Stanley Wood House, was sent by the lady of the house in 1909 to tell her son, away on holiday, that a dozen chicks had hatched from his eggs. The house was demolished and Little Reeves Avenue built over its site in 1960.

STANLEY WOOD HOUSE

On the edge of Amersham Common, Raans Farm was built in about 1540 on the site of the former Raans Manor House. The owners originally farmed part of the common land as well as their own, which included cleared woodland on the slope of the Chess Valley. The Chesham railway line now forms a barrier between the farm's fields and the houses of both Amersham on the Hill and Amersham Common. Both views were published in about 1912, the upper showing the farmhouse and the lower showing part of the footpath from White Lion Road and the hedge which forms the boundary between the farm and the field later used by Boughton's for the open-air seasoning of timber for the Ercol chair factory in High Wycombe.

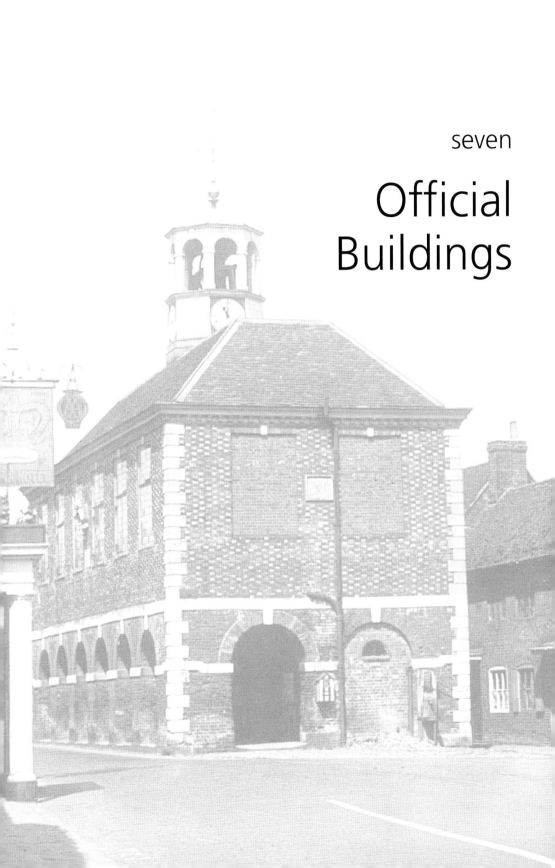

seven

Official
Buildings

Amersham's first post office, pictured here in the early 1900s, was in the High Street where, in 1830, Francis Priest combined the duties of postmaster with his trade of boot and shoe maker, and was also parish clerk. John Bettsworth followed him from about 1840-70, and in the 1860s doubled as schoolmaster. Emily Bettsworth then followed on from her father until the end of the century.

When Amersham on the Hill's main post office opened in 1931, the old town office was downgraded to a sub office and moved three doors along the road towards the Market Hall. Pictured in the mid-1930s with a flock of sheep making their leisurely way along the High Street, the new office, in Elsie Pratt's tobacconists shop, is beyond Lloyds Bank just behind the first parked car.

Thomas Matthews, in White Lion Road, was Amersham Common's first sub postmaster. Emily Passmore was in charge of both the grocer's shop and post office when, in 1907, Amersham Common telephone exchange opened in the same premises. The office is at the right of this postcard, published in about 1915 after Ada Smith had taken over. In 1930 the post office and the telephone exchange, then renamed Little Chalfont, moved to new premises nearer the station.

In 1930, Rhodes Stores, in this new block of shops adjacent to the station, became Little Chalfont's sub post office and telephone exchange. This 1935 postcard includes the post office with a pillar box on the pavement outside, between The Rendezvous, where Mrs Bedfer sold tobacco, confectionery and newspapers, and Swannell & Sly's estate agency in the small annexe to the main building.

The first sub post office in the new town opened in about 1900 in the sweet shop on the left of this 1910 view of the upper part of Station Road. The sweet shop later became an unofficial tuck-shop for the pupils of the grammar school at the top of Station Road. The Station Hotel's garden extended behind the hedge on the opposite side of the road. The office was run in conjunction with the neighbouring Temperance Hotel, initially by Henrietta Blake. Herbert Smith followed in 1905, then Laura Nevell, who remained in charge until the office closed.

Opposite above: Replacing the old town office, Amersham on the Hill's main post office opened in Chesham Road in 1931. Next door to the post office was a private house, then Foster's Garage, beyond which a vacant site extended up the hill to the trees at Oakfield Corner, all pictured in the mid-1930s.

Opposite below: In 1961 the post office moved to new premises built in the last remaining space on the east side of Hill Avenue. The post office building is set back from the general building line in the centre of this 1996 photograph looking up Hill Avenue. It was, by then, only a delivery office, as the post office counter had moved again into a shop at Oakfield Corner.

Old Amersham's most familiar building, pictured from the High Street in 1915, is the Market Hall (often called the Town Hall), which restricts traffic flow in the centre of the main street. Built in 1682, at the expense of the Drake family, with an upstairs meeting hall over an open piazza, it was the venue for the Tuesday charter market, which died out in the nineteenth century.

Here an artist is painting the view of the High Street from under the Market Hall in 1925. To her right, a second staircase to the hall had been built across the end arch some ten years earlier, following the 1911 Public Safety Act. Over the centuries, the hall accommodated the parish school, the petty sessions court, penny readings and magic lantern shows, local society meetings and various charity events.

Looking at the Market Hall from Market Square in 1930, one arch is blocked by the original lock-up, with the 1785 town pump in front of it and the main staircase to the hall behind. The Drake family arms are displayed on the street side of the hall, which is surmounted by a turret and a clock visible over the rooftops. It is said that the bosses of the brewery wanted the north face of the clock covered to prevent their men clock-watching.

Whielden, Amersham.

G.Ward. 117.

Amersham's first true workhouse, where the poor were accommodated and not just employed, opened in about 1780 in an early seventeenth-century building in Whielden Street, remaining there until the Amersham Union Workhouse opened further along the road. Pictured in 1910, when part had become shop premises, the workhouse is the tall building on the right with four dormer windows.

Opposite above: Pictured in about 1930, the Poor Law Institution for the Amersham Union of Parishes, an impressive Tudor-style building designed by Bucks-born architect George Gilbert Scott in 1838, opened to receive inmates in the following year. The infirmary wing, to the right of the main buildings, was added in 1906 and became St Mary's Hospital in 1924.

Opposite below: When war was declared in 1939, the Amersham Union building, clearly displaying '1838 A.U.' over the central arch, was taken over and, augmented by a range of temporary huts, became an emergency services hospital. Staffed mainly by students from St Mary's Hospital in Paddington, it was intended to take overspill from there during air raids. After the war, under the NHS, it became Amersham General Hospital.

"St Marys Hospital. & Institute Amersham" WHA 5796

Sycamore Corner, Amersham.

Pictured here in the 1950s, the end shop behind the direction signpost had been used for various official purposes since the beginning of the Second World War. Initially housing both National Registration and Food Offices, and later the local Customs and Excise Office, when photographed it was the base for the Women's Voluntary Service and Civil Defence organisations.

eight

Transport

Above: In the early twentieth century, travelling usually meant walking or horse riding. This 1910 scene includes two gentlemen on their way along White Lion Road towards Amersham town. This country road, running in a straight line near the railway, already bears an early sign of modernity, a line of telegraph poles and wires carrying services to and from the telephone exchange in Amersham Common post office.

Left: This pony and trap, pictured in 1928 outside the Eagle pub, was a familiar sight throughout Amersham town as Tom Baker delivered bread from his High Street bakery to the local residents. The loaves were carried from house to house in the wicker basket, replenished from stock carried under sacks behind the driver's seat.

MISSENDEN AND RICKMANSWORTH COACH. 1911.

Although regular stage-coach services through Amersham had ceased in the nineteenth century, they were revived as a tourist attraction before the Great War and again in the 1920s, running from Wendover and Missenden through Amersham to either Rickmansworth or Windsor. Pictured in the Broadway in 1911, this four-horse coach is speeding on its way to Rickmansworth after a brief stop at the Crown Hotel.

Horses were employed on some types of heavy haulage work until well into the motor era. Here a team of four shire horses is pictured in the late 1920s, hauling tree trunks probably destined for one of the local chair factories. They are seen passing Pipers Wood, opposite the end of Shardeloes Park on the Missenden Road.

The amount of horse traffic had a serious effect on the poorly-surfaced roads, and Amersham's main street was described as a dust bowl in dry weather and a quagmire after rain, as seen here in 1905 in Market Square. These conditions made it very unpleasant for pedestrians.

Conditions for those on foot were improved a few years later with the first pedestrian crossings, stone paths raised slightly above the general road surface. The High Street is shown here in 1912, looking west past the Kings Arms on the left and the Red Lion on the right, with a crossing connecting the two pavements for those who wished to patronise both sides.

Above: After 1900 bicycles became a popular means of local transport, and the two girls on this 1905 postcard are examining a shiny modern machine. At this date Amersham boasted two cycle dealers, both of which actually made their own machines, selling for up to fifteen guineas each. This was a considerable outlay for the average worker, when even the headmaster of the new grammar school was only paid £5 per week.

Right: Cycles also came into their own for local deliveries of lightweight goods, and this late 1920s photograph features the delivery boy from Pisces fish shop with a typical delivery cycle, somewhere on his round in Amersham on the Hill.

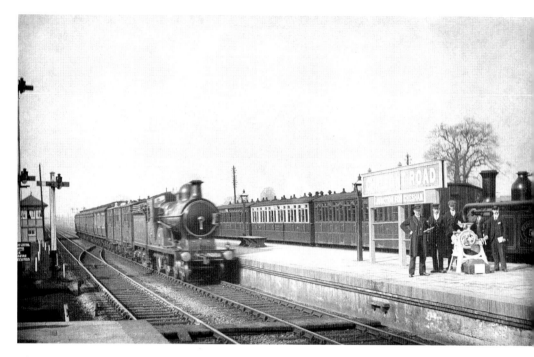

The Metropolitan Railway reached Chalfont Road, which was then only a road junction among a few farms and scattered cottages, in 1889. The line then continued as a single track across Amersham Common and steeply down into the Chess Valley to the terminus at Chesham. Passengers for Amersham transferred at Chalfont Road to a connecting horse-bus service for the thirty-five-minute journey to The Griffin. The line to Amersham and on to Aylesbury was opened three years later and the line to Chesham then became a branch off the main through service, with a single train shunting up and down the hill all day. In this 1900 photograph of Chalfont Road Station, the Chesham 'shuttle' stands at the bay platform as a London-bound train from Aylesbury pulls into the station.

Opposite above: The south side of Chalfont Road station is shown here in the early years of the twentieth century, when the only entrance was on the far side. Even after the station was renamed Chalfont & Latimer in 1915 to emphasise a wider catchment area, there was still no direct access from this side. A footpath entrance was created in 1927 and the road Station Approach a further six years later.

Opposite below: Photographed from Bell Lane Bridge, the steam-hauled three-coach train from Chesham heads toward Chalfont & Latimer on a summer evening in 1958, two years before the electrification of the line. The single-track branch here runs between the twin-track main line and Boughton's engineering works.

This picture of Amersham & Chesham Bois station dates from about 1930. The joint Metropolitan and Great Central Railway had reached Amersham in 1892, prompting the development of Amersham on the Hill. Thirty years later, the station name was temporarily altered to include the neighbouring village, which was also growing into a high-class residential area but was not directly served by any railway.

Steam-rollers and traction engines were a common sight in Amersham on their way from Boughtons of Amersham Common to work for local authorities and road builders throughout Buckinghamshire and many neighbouring counties. In this photograph, Alice, one of Boughton's Fowler compound rollers, is working on a local site.

Tom Baker's wife and two of their children pose with his motorcycle and side-car outside his bakery in 1928, when such machines were still quite rare. The view includes Bailey's antique shop behind them on the other side of a traffic-free High Street.

Amersham's first petrol station was at the Griffin Hotel, the tall building near the centre of this 1926 view, where a kerb-side pump dispensing Pratt's Golden Motor Oil was installed in 1920. When pictured, the Griffin Garage in the yard behind the hotel was advertised as 'automobile engineers, stockists of petrol, oil, tyres and accessories' and undertook 'repairs of all descriptions'.

As private motoring became more widespread, car dealers and petrol stations opened in most towns, and William Foster Ltd, who started business in 1910 as cycle makers in Chesham, had recently opened this garage in Chesham Road when this picture was taken in 1930. They were agents for the superior cars by Rover and Humber, and offered a choice of four brands of fuel: Shell, BP, Texaco and Pratt's Commercial.

Right: By the end of the 1920s, although cycles were still much in evidence, motors were becoming commonplace, and any area off the main traffic routes could become an unofficial car park for visitors to the old town. Here, seen from the Market Hall arch, four drivers have chosen to park their vehicles in the Market Square beside the end cottage of Church Row.

Below: The Amersham & District Motor Bus and Haulage Company was founded in 1919 and started business with two solid-tyred buses running between Chesham and High Wycombe via Amersham, where their base was the yard of the Griffin. Business grew rapidly, and ten years later they were operating a dozen routes with a fleet of thirty buses from a proper garage at the end of Broadway. In 1931 they also introduced an hourly service to London using AEC Regal coaches, one of which is pictured here the following year outside their garage, which still stands today as a car showroom, on the edge of Dovecotes Meadow.

AMERSHAM – MARKET SQUARE.

In 1933, Amersham's bus company and most other private bus operators around London were absorbed into the London Passenger Transport Board who, in 1935, built a larger garage, bearing the familiar L.T. roundel, adjoining the old one. This photograph shows a selection of buses waiting outside the new garage, with its separate enquiry office and accommodation wing to the right, where the Tesco petrol station stands today.

London Transport started using double-deckers on their busiest country bus routes, but the 336 service to Watford had to wait until the introduction of the RLH low-bridge class of double-decker bus which was able to pass under Blackhorse Bridge, on the road between Amersham on the Hill and Little Chalfont. In this 1950 photograph, the first of the new buses passes under the bridge with only a few inches to spare.

nine

Recreation

Harvest Time at Amersham.

Walking is a form of healthy recreation that was particularly popular in a beautiful rural area such as the Chilterns. In this 1925 view of the field behind Amersham church, a small group is setting off on one of the most familiar local footpaths, linking the old town with the new. It involves a climb across the cornfield and into Rectory Wood toward the crest of the hill, but the reward is an excellent view over Old Amersham.

More strenuous walking or hiking, usually in organised groups, was particularly popular in the 1920s and '30s. This group has arrived at the main Amersham to High Wycombe road via the field path from Penn Street, and is waiting before starting across the road to Woodrow or along to Mop End. Their leader is standing by a Bucks County Council road sign on which the distance to Woodrow has been obliterated.

Cycling is another good way of seeing the countryside and here, in the 1930s, half a dozen young men have parked their machines against the kerb outside The Kings Arms, either to obtain refreshment there or to purchase cycle accessories or spare parts from George Ward's shop almost next door.

Another rural pastime is hunting, and here the hounds of the Old Berkeley (West) Hunt are assembling in Shardeloes Park for one of their regular meets. Not all the riders or their horses were local, because in the 1900s the Metropolitan Railway attached horse-box wagons to certain trains from Finchley Road on hunt days, charging only twice the ordinary fare for those London riders who wished to bring their mounts with them.

Williams   Tommy   Hull   Osborne   Bright   Tom   Rocky

2/13 Bradley Gdns
West Ealing

My dear Alice
Can you
come up to tea
tomorrow afternoon
if you are not
otherwise engaged
Do not trouble
to write either
way. What do
you think of this
famous team. Guess

Redrup.   Bob   Reg   Isham

AMERSHAM FOOTBALL TEAM, 1903.

Amersham Town Football Club was founded in 1890, initially playing on Barn Meadow and using the adjacent National School for changing rooms, with The Eagle as their headquarters. The team pictured here in 1902 had been the previous season's champions in the Wycombe & District Combination League. Although postal rules had changed in 1900 to permit messages on the address side of postcards, the sender of this card still used the picture side.

BADMINTON COURT HOTEL
AMERSHAM.

Once a coaching inn called Rumseys, this house in Church Street became the offices for Weller's brewery. After the brewery closed, it was converted, in 1931, into a badminton hall where county matches were played. In 1935 it was reconditioned as The Badminton Court Hotel, with 'Running hot and cold water in bedrooms, private bathrooms, lounge, large garden, and garage', but closed in 1950.

Right: This building, at the end of Station Parade, opened in 1907 as the Bijou Hall, for lectures, dances and concerts. It was converted in 1922 to the Pavilion Cinema & Café, 'combining the acme of comfort with the essence of cinematographic art'. In 1936 it became the 240-seat Playhouse Theatre, and remained open, with a short break and change of management, until 1957. This was their advertisement in 1951.

Below: The Regent Cinema, which was built by a local firm, opened in Sycamore Road in 1928, and was described then as the finest cinema in Bucks, with a luxuriously appointed interior. When first built, it was by far the largest building in the new town, incongruously situated between private houses and an open space, and facing a pair of mature elm trees across the road.

Playhouse Theatre

AMERSHAM REPERTORY COMPANY
under the direction of
ROSA DE LEON and JOHN FERRIS

Times of Performances :
Tuesday 8.00 : Wednesday 2.45 and 7.00 : Thursday 7.00
Friday 8.00 : Saturday 2.45, 6.00 and 8.30.

Prices : 5 -, 4 -, 3 , 2 -.   **All Seats Bookable**
Box Office open 10 a.m.—9 p.m.

TELEPHONE 994

STATION ROAD · AMERSHAM

In the 1920s little excuse was needed for a parade or other social gathering, and this photograph, from the Baker's family album, shows their son and daughters with a friend outside the bakery, all dressed up for Amersham's May Day celebrations in 1928.

By ancient charter, Amersham held two annual fairs: on Whit Monday for cattle and on 19 September, the birthday of the parish church's patron saint, for hiring workers. In the twentieth century, the cattle fair died out completely and the hiring fair changed to an amusement fair, extended to two days. One of the largest sideshows was Pelham's steam-driven three-abreast gallopers, pictured here in the 1950s.

ten

Events

Around the beginning of the twentieth century, the main event in Amersham's social calendar was the August flower show and fête. Until 1905, it was held in Dovecotes Meadow, between Broadway and the river. Pictured in 1904, a horse-drawn vehicle made up to look like a state carriage, and carrying members of the band, stands in Broadway outside the gasworks' gate. The flower show marquee and the funfair's swingboats are visible over the wall of Line's coachbuilding works.

From 1906 onwards the flower show was held in Rectory Meadow, from where the brewery chimneys can be seen to the left of the trees on this 1907 postcard. The flower tent was just one of the many attractions, which also included a roundabout, swingboats, coconut shy, a puppet booth and other sideshows. The town band is grouped in a circle near the top of the sloping field, awaiting the appearance of their conductor.

As part of an army exercise in October 1907, a large contingent of troops set up camp in Shardeloes park. In the upper photograph there are hundreds of horses, but barely a dozen men visible outside the tents. The lower picture, a closer view of part of the encampment, was posted by one of the soldiers to his wife in Aylesbury, telling her that he was greatly improving his skill at diabolo as he had plenty of spare time to practise, also that on the day of writing it was pouring with rain and there was hardly anyone about.

On 17 May 1910 the official proclamation of the accession of King George V was made from the arch of the Market Hall. Here a crowd of local residents, some using their carts and carriages as grandstands, gather in Market Square to witness the occasion.

Among Amersham's events to celebrate King George's Coronation in 1911 was a fancy-dress parade. This decorated carriage carrying 'John Bull' and his wife Mary, which won second prize in its class is standing outside the fire station. When needed, the horse-drawn engine was manned by Captain Darlington and his team of twelve men, whose first job was to round up the horses to pull the engine to the fire.

These two views, from opposite sides of Market Square, show the crowds celebrating the April 1914 election of William du Pré as Tory Member of Parliament for the South Bucks constituency, a seat he retained until defeated by a Liberal in 1923. The first floor of the old school was du Pré's local headquarters for the election campaign and its frontage is covered with posters announcing: 'Home rule means separation' and 'The Land Union's Caution to Amersham's Rural Landowners' as well as the obvious 'Vote for du Pré'.

During the First World War, a battalion of the King's Royal Rifle Corps which had been flooded out of Halton Camp was billetted in Amersham, where they used Pondwicks, the field between the maltings and Church Street, as a drill ground. On 18 November 1914 a Royal Inspection took place and in the upper photograph the men, led by their band, are marching from Church Street into Market Square on their way to take up their places for the inspection. In the lower photo, the royal car carrying King George V proceeds slowly along the High Street between the smartly assembled ranks of soldiers and the less organised groups of local residents.

Also in 1914, fundraising events were organised to help the Belgian refugees who had fled to England when the Germans invaded their home country. Here the town band leads a procession of Amersham folk in fancy dress past Turpins Row on their way to a comic football match in aid of the Belgian Fund.

At Whitsun 1915, the Amersham Scout Band leads a column of troops out of town at the start of a route-march, watched by a few locals, including the sender of the postcard (on the pavement, wearing a straw hat).

In September 1922, the members and supporters of the Old Berkeley Hunt gathered in The Broadway for the meet, filling the road with a wide assortment of cars, vans, and trucks.

Opposite above and below: Amersham's memorial to those who fell in the Second World War is the Garden of Remembrance alongside the churchyard, containing the 1914–18 war memorial moved from its original position close to the church. In the upper photograph, representatives of military and civilian groups are assembled in the new gardens in September 1949 for the service of dedication. Pictured below, Sir Bernard Paget unveiled a tablet on the wall of the garden, listing the names of the Amersham men and women who died in the service of their country.

Other local titles published by Tempus

Beaconsfield

COLIN J. SEABRIGHT

Compiled with 200 archive images, this detailed volume illustrates just how much Beaconsfield has changed over the last century. The selection includes vistas of well-known streets like London Road, Warwick Road, Ledborough Lane and Penn Road, alongside postcard views of shops, places of worship, schools, public houses and historic inns. Sporting activities, royal visits and local people are also recorded.

0 7524 3093 9

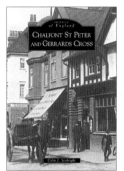

Chalfont St Peter and Gerrards Cross

COLIN J. SEABRIGHT

Illustrated with over 200 photographs and postcards, this fascinating collection captures the twentieth-century history of the two adjacent villages of Chalfont St Peter and Gerrards Cross – from the shops and businesses that evolved from the market village of Chalfont St Peter, to the rapid growth and development of Gerrards Cross into a thriving commuter village, which came with the opening of the railway in 1906.

0 7524 2493 9

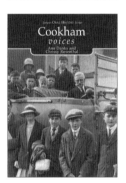

Cookham Voices

ANN DANKS AND CHRISSY ROSENTHAL

This volume is a vivid and moving record chronicling the many voices of Cookham over the years. Childhood recollections of the schoolroom, hall dances, tin baths and gas lamps feature alongside various memorable village characters. There are reminders of harsher times, of war and rationing, and also of safer and friendlier times in a village where everyone knew each other by name.

0 7524 2656 7

Royal Grammar School, High Wycombe

J.I. MITCHELL

The Royal Grammar School, High Wycombe, will celebrate the 450th anniversary of its royal charter in 2012. Though pictures of the original Hospital of St John have not survived, this book provides a pictorial history of its successor, the town's grammar school, from the mid-nineteenth century to the present day. This collection will be of interest to pupils, staff, former students and anyone with an affection for High Wycombe and its story.

0 7524 2861 6

If you are interested in purchasing other books published by Tempus, or in case you have difficulty finding any Tempus books in your local bookshop, you can also place orders directly through our website

www.tempus-publishing.com

or from   **BOOKPOST**, Freepost, PO Box 29, Douglas, Isle of Man, IM99 1BQ
tel 01624 836000   email bookshop@enterprise.net